Pr

by

_____

on

_____

John the Baptist

Matthew 3:1-17; Mark 1:1-11; Luke 3:1-22

John was Jesus' cousin. John lived alone out in the desert. He wore rough and simple clothes. He ate the food he found in the desert.

God had given John a special job. John told the people, "Get ready! God will soon send the Savior!" John talked near the Jordan River. People came from all the towns to listen!

John told people, "Stop doing wrong. Ask God to forgive you. Do what is right!"

The people asked, "What should we do?"

John said, "If you have two coats, give one to a person who has NO coat. If you have food, give some to HUNGRY people."

Some soldiers asked John, "What should WE do?"

John said, "Be honest. Don't take money that isn't yours. Be happy with what you have."

John baptized many people in the river. Being baptized showed a person wanted God to forgive the wrong things he or she did. One day, Jesus asked John to baptize HIM. John said, "YOU should baptize ME!" But Jesus said, "No. This is what God wants us to do. And I want to obey God."

So John baptized Jesus. Then God's Spirit, looking like a dove, came down from heaven to Jesus. God spoke from heaven. "This is My Son. I love Him. I am pleased with Him!"

Jesus Chooses Helpers

Matthew 4:18-22; Luke 5:27-28; 6:12-16; 9:1-6

Jesus walked by the Sea of Galilee. He saw fishermen throwing big fishing nets out into the water. Jesus called, "Peter! Andrew! Come, follow Me. I'll teach you how to tell people about God." The two men gladly went with Jesus!

Jesus walked on down the shore. He saw two other fishermen in a boat. "James and John!" Jesus called. "Come with Me!" James and John also went with Jesus. Now Jesus had FOUR helpers!

Later, Jesus saw a man named Matthew.
Matthew was working, collecting money.
"Follow Me, Matthew," said Jesus. Matthew
got right up and went with Jesus. Now Jesus
had FIVE friends to help Him!

Jesus asked more people to follow Him—six, seven, eight, nine, ten, eleven, twelve helpers! Jesus taught His 12 helpers many things about God's love. Jesus' helpers told other people what they'd learned about God's love!

Nicodemus and Jesus

John 3:1-17

Nicodemus was a leader who wanted to know more about Jesus. One quiet night, Nicodemus came to see Jesus. He said, "Jesus, we know You came from God. No one else can do what You do!"

Jesus told Nicodemus that he needed to be born
again. Nicodemus didn't understand Jesus' words.
But Jesus explained that Nicodemus had to be
born into God's family.

"God loves this world very much," Jesus said. "That's why He sent Me here. I am God's very own Son. When a person believes in Me, that person gets to be part of God's family now and forever!"

The Woman at the Well

John 4:3-42

Jesus and His helpers walked and walked.
They walked until it was noon. They were
hot, hungry and tired.

They stopped at a town to rest. Jesus' friends went to buy food. Jesus sat by the well just outside of the town.

A woman came to get water from the well.
Jesus asked her for a drink. She was surprised
Jesus would talk to her. Then Jesus surprised
her even more! He told about many things she
had done.

She was amazed. Jesus knew all about her! The woman said, "When the Savior comes, He'll talk to us like You are talking to me."

Jesus told her, "I AM the Savior God promised to send!"

The woman was VERY excited! She ran back into the town shouting, "Listen! There's a Man by the well. I think He's the SAVIOR God promised to send!"

Jesus knows what you are like and what you do. He loves you!

Many people came to meet Jesus for themselves! They listened to His words. They asked Him to tell them more about God's love! They told the woman, "You were right. Jesus IS the Savior God promised to send!"

Jesus Loves Children

Matthew 19:13-15; Mark 10:13-16

Some families were going to see Jesus. The parents wanted Jesus to pray for their children.

The families walked and walked. Parents carried tired little ones. No one wanted to stop! When they saw a crowd of people, they asked, "Is Jesus here?" He was!

The families hurried to where Jesus was!
But as they got close to Jesus, Jesus' friends
stepped in their way. The men said, "STOP!
Don't bother Jesus. He is too BUSY to see
children. Go away!"

The children and parents were sad. Slowly, they turned to leave.

But Jesus saw what was happening. Jesus was NOT happy! He said to His friends, "Let the children COME to Me! NEVER tell them to go away. God's kingdom belongs to ones like these!"

Jesus loves you. He wants to be your friend.

Then Jesus motioned for the children. They ran to Him! He took them in His arms and held them. He prayed for them. Jesus was NOT too busy for the children. He didn't want them to go away! Jesus LOVES children!

Jesus Loves Zacchaeus

Luke 19:1-10

Zacchaeus was a tax collector. People did NOT like him much. He took more money than was fair. And taking that money made him RICH.

Zacchaeus heard that Jesus was coming. He
wanted to SEE Jesus! But Zacchaeus was very
short. He could NEVER see over all the people
in a crowd.

So Zacchaeus ran AHEAD of the crowd. He climbed up into a tree! Now he was taller than ANYONE!

When Jesus walked right under that tree, He
STOPPED. He looked up, right at Zacchaeus!
He said, "Zacchaeus, please come down. I must
stay at your house today!"

Zacchaeus hurried down the tree. WOW! Jesus was coming to HIS house! The people in the crowd grumbled, "Zacchaeus is such a bad man. Why is Jesus going with HIM?"

We can say we're sorry when we do wrong. Jesus will forgive us and help us do right.

Zacchaeus looked at Jesus. He wanted to show he had CHANGED! He said, "Look, Lord! Here and now, I give half of what I own to poor people. And if I have cheated anyone, I will pay them back FOUR TIMES what I took!"

Jesus said, "Today God's salvation has come to Zacchaeus's house!"